Life In The Sea

Written by Eileen Curran

Illustrated by Joel Snyder

Troll Associates

Library of Congress Cataloging in Publication Data

Curran, Eileen.
  Life in the sea.

    Summary: Introduces some of the animals and fishes that
live in the ocean.
        1. Marine fauna—Juvenile literature.   2. Marine
flora—Juvenile literature.   [1. Marine animals]
I. Snyder, Joel, ill.   II. Title.
QL122.2.C87   1985   591.92   84-16190
ISBN 0-8167-0448-1 (lib. bdg.)
ISBN 0-8167-0449-X (pbk.)

The ocean is a big place.

Whose home could it be?
Let's go down to the water.

Let's go down to the sea.

Let's watch a sea gull...

and a flying fish.

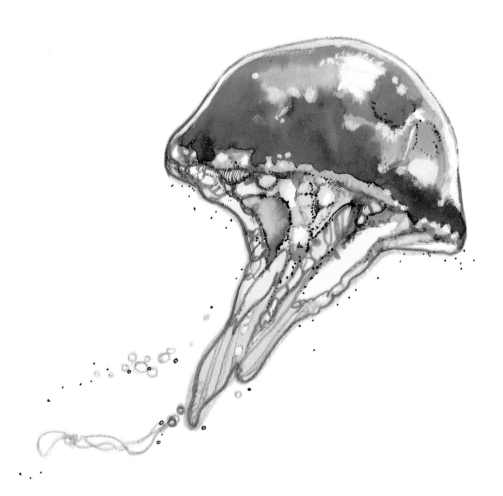

Who lives in the ocean?
A jellyfish lives there.

And so does a crab.

KELP

BUTTERFLY FISH

Look, a tiny fish is hiding.

SEA ANEMONE

ROCK WEED

It is hiding near the seaweed.

Who else lives in the sea?

DOG SNAPPERS

Do you see this school of fish?
How many do you see?

Here comes a sea horse.

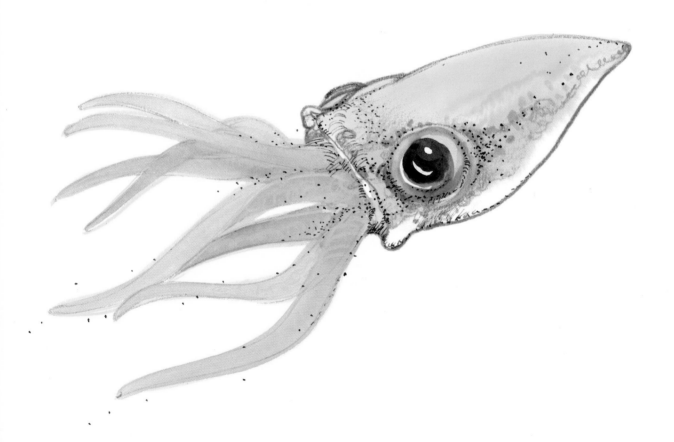

Away goes a squid.

SPINY SEA URCHIN

The sea urchin lives here.

MANTA RAY

SEA PERCH

And so does a ray.
Do you see the school of fish?
How many do you see?

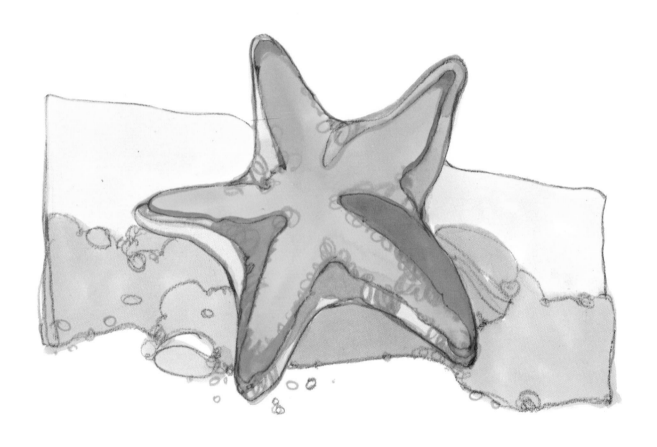

Off goes a starfish.
Most starfish have five arms.

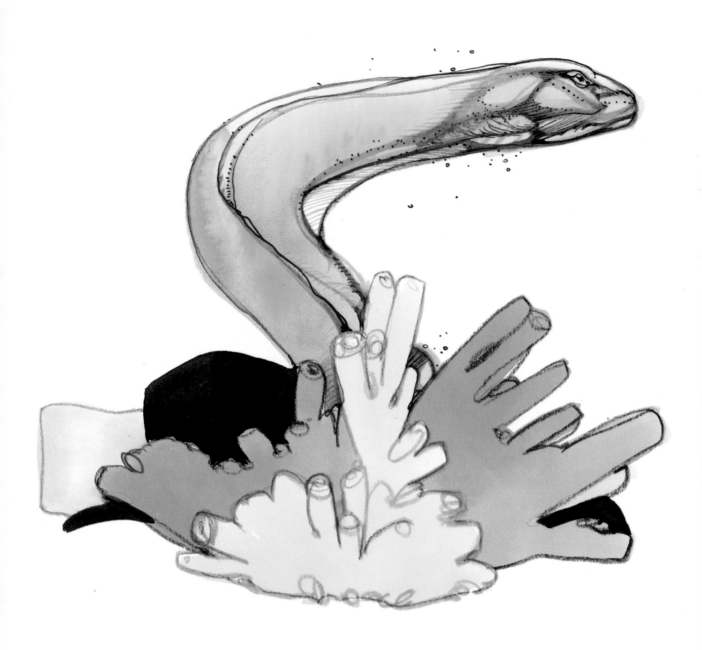

Why is the eel hiding?

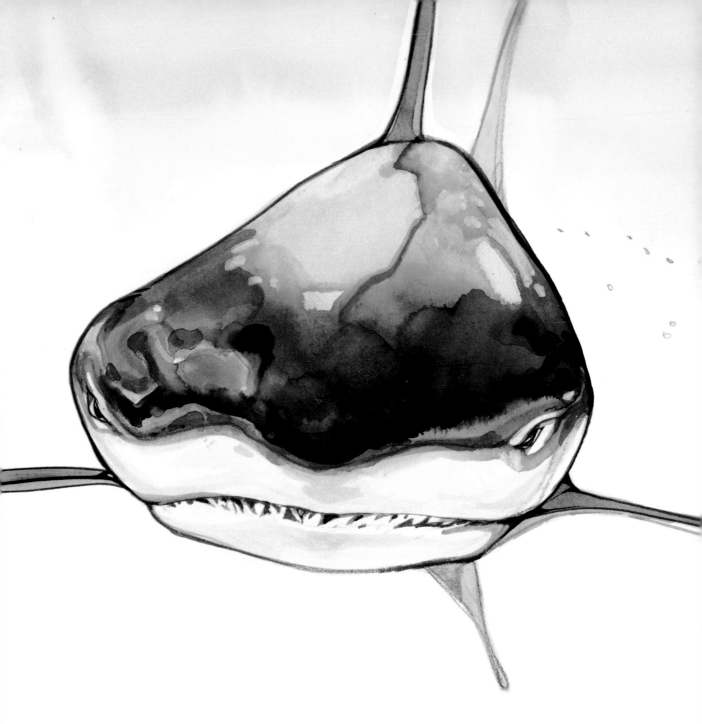

Now you know.
Here comes the shark.

GROUPERS

What else lives in the sea?

CORAL

BLOWFISH

SKATE-EGG CAPSULE

What else lives here?

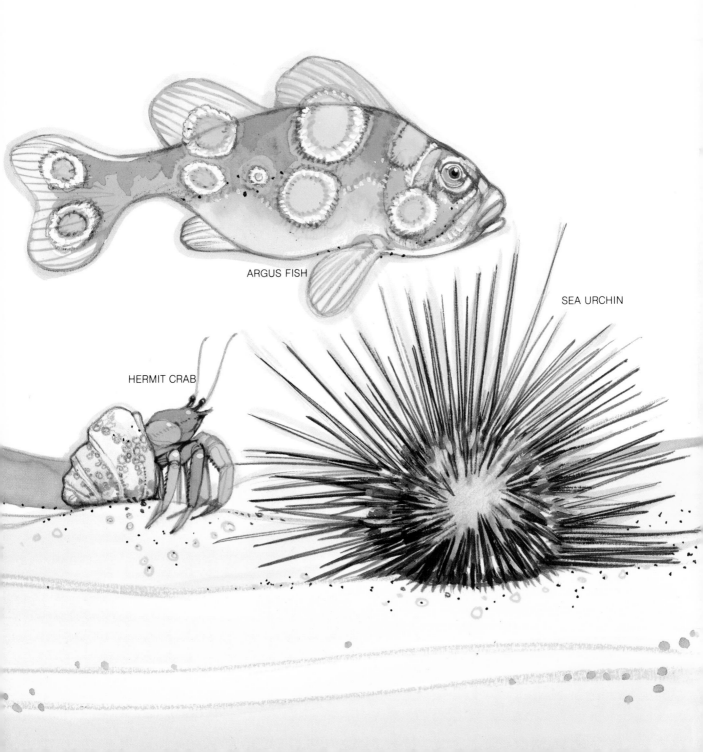

ARGUS FISH

SEA URCHIN

HERMIT CRAB

Here comes an octopus.

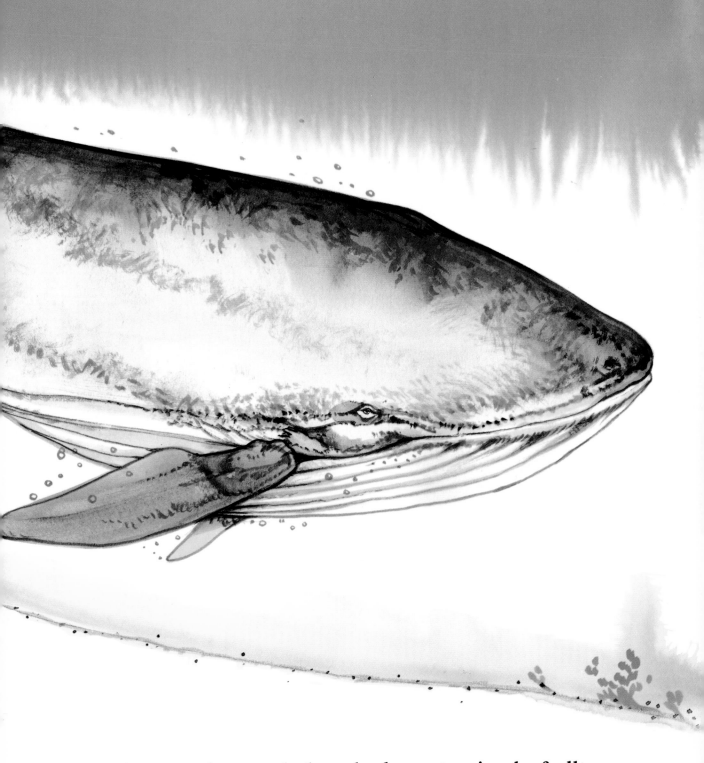

Away swims a whale—the largest animal of all.

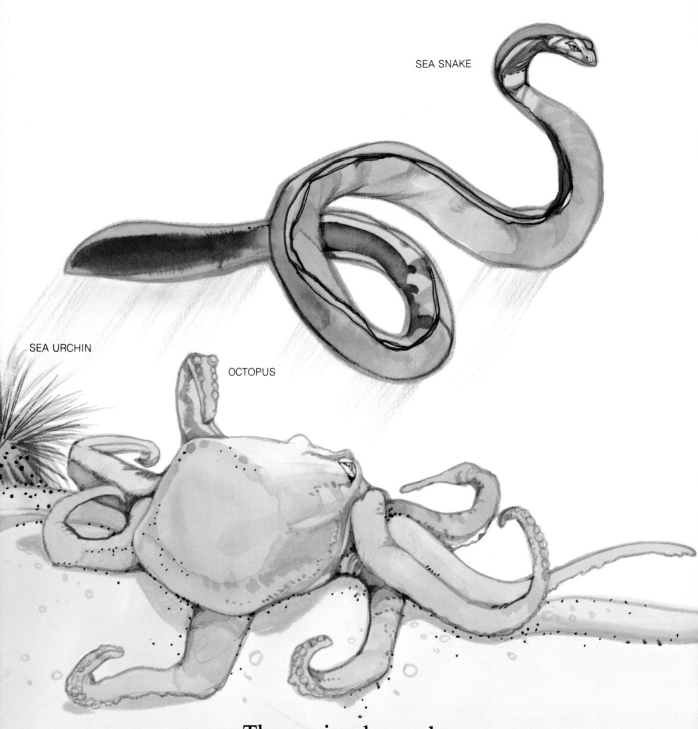

SEA SNAKE

SEA URCHIN

OCTOPUS

The sea is a busy place.

SHARK

CORAL

CORAL

YELLOW JACKS

STING RAY

Whose home can it be?

It is a home for playful dolphins.
It is a home for fish and plants and
many special creatures.

What a wonderful place it can be!